Charred Horses

Jon Ferry

Charred Horses Copyright © 2017 by Jon Ferry.

Published by Prominence Publishing

www.prominencepublishing.com

ISBN: 978-1-988925-08-0

First Edition: November 2017

Table of Contents

Dedication

To my wife Rosalind, son William and family... and all the tired horses in the sun.

Foreword

A dear friend said the other day he often wondered how you define poetry: "Do you just know it when you hear/read it?"

Well, I think that's as good a definition as any. At least it's a good starting point.

As has often been noted, the word poetry derives from the Greek "poein," meaning "to make." Which is why Idaho-born poet Ezra Pound famously referred to fellow poet T.S. Eliot as "il miglior fabbro" or "the better maker." More highfalutin definitions of poetry abound, such as the one at Dictionary.com: "The art of rhythmical composition, written or spoken, for exciting pleasure by beautiful, imaginative, or elevated thoughts." Elevated thoughts? Often, too elevated. The fact is a lot of modern poetry is so elevated it strikes out. It's as if its makers were frightened their poems might be too approachable, too people-friendly... too easy to understand.

I think poems should be readable. You shouldn't have to be a high-powered academic or crossword addict to disentangle them. But they should also be creative and imaginative, and shouldn't simply re-work well-worn themes. "Make it new," was how Pound put it in his oft-recycled slogan.

Great poems are rare, but you know them almost instantly. They invariably have meaning, emotion, color, rhythm, music and soul. They move you ... and become your friend for life.

The wonderful poem by W.B. Yeats titled "An Irish Airman Foresees His Death" certainly qualifies as one. You just know it when you hear/read it.

My goal in this collection, though, is not quite so ambitious. I simply want to speak directly to you about things that I think might interest you. Thank you for listening/reading.

Jon Ferry, North Vancouver, 2017

Charred horses

The Four Horsemen of the Apocalypse
have left the stables in their chariots.
White, red, black and sickly pale,
their steeds run like latter-day Secretariats.

The Last Days appear round the corner,
and we're all becoming more aware
of the forces massing on our borders.
Nature and nurture are on a terrible tear.

Fire and floods are spitting fury.
A total solar eclipse has everybody stirred.
War continues to ravage the Middle East.
Terrorism unhinges the "developed" world.

But the image that tears the heart out,
that truly brings the calamity home,
is of carcasses of charred horses
trapped in a burnt British Columbia pine grove.

Like moose and other vulnerable wildlife,
those 10 horses failed to outrun the wildfires
sweeping through western North America,
turning its life-giving forests into funeral pyres.

Native Indian chiefs explain how they've lived
with free-roaming horses for hundreds of years.
They say they plan to use them as backup transport,
if the planet's economic engine disappears.

The sun blackens, the trumpets blow;
the Second Coming is drawing nigh.
I hear the neighing of nervous wild horses.
Or is it just the thunder in the sky?

The spirit owl

An owl flew into our balcony the other night,
giving me and my wife a terrible fright.
The Northern Saw-Whet Owl was rather small,
but it was clear it'd taken a nasty fall.

My wife picked up the owl and kept it warm
to ensure there was no enduring harm.
Its feathered body and yellow eyes
were a fluffy brown bundle of great prize.

She laid it in an upturned cowboy hat
where it soon morphed into an acrobat,
swiveling around its upright head
as if it were returning from the dead.

It plumped up its body, shook its tail,
then leapt up onto the balcony rail
and looked me directly in the eye,
before flying off in search of other prey.

Some say the owl is the wisest bird,
others feel it an animal to be feared.
Certainly, it's known as a fortune forecaster
warning humans of death or disaster.

I believe owls are agents of change
in a world that's out of our range
and rarely intersects with ours,
despite having supernatural powers.

I also think the owl came to us that night
may have taken a wrong turn in its flight.
It may also have wished to let us know
a little about what makes the winds blow.

I hope to meet it again some morning
when we can learn more about its warning --
and about how we humans see only a slice
of what happens in the spirit life.

Freedom has its limits

Some people prefer freedom and wide open spaces.
Others crave fences and boundaries, even if it's only a hill or stream.
For some, the words tumble out like carbonated water.
Others yearn for the structure of a stanza or other metrical scheme.

Some are drawn to all-you-can eat restaurants,
others to strict diets that promise to make the colon pristine.
For neat freaks, the day must be chopped up into regular segments.
Red-blooded dreamers hate anything that seems so routine.

I like to think that human possibilities are endless,
that all you have to do to thrive is open your eyes.
But any time I view the mirror, I'm reminded we all
need definition and a limit-less life is distinctly unwise.

Moving into the light

As ancient Greek philosopher Heraclitus explained,
everything is in motion, nothing is constrained.
The earth's climate is always on the move,
it's never stuck in some muddy groove.

Activists like to wield anti-development signs,
smoke weed and listen to wind chimes.
But if our economy isn't on course to grow,
it's shrinking, and out of work we go.

Neutrality and balance have a certain cachet.
But just ask the folks in Holland and Norway
how being neutral worked in World War Two.
If you're not beating someone, they're beating you.

Nature, as Tennyson said, is red in tooth and claw.
You're better off being rich than poor.
So dust off your boots and make your stand.
Show others the path to the promised land.

Some people tend to sidle away from debate.
Others, like Stylite monks, prefer a static state.
But if, in fact, we're hard-wired for life atop a pillar,
what on earth do we have arms and legs for?

Meditation and yoga are fine to calm the nerves.
So is eating vegan appetizers for hors d'oeuvres.
It's hard, though, to see how they work well,
if you're trying vainly to bust out of your shell.

At some point, we simply have to leave the cave
and roll the big rock blocking our airway.
We have to exercise our undying human right
not to cringe and cower from the light.

Cravings

I write this poem not because
I'm especially vain or hanker for fame,
but because this is what I like to do
when I can't think of doing anything better.

I do it the way some people cook,
not so much to feed themselves
or their friends, but because they have
this urge to scratch a recurring itch.

I do what I do with words because,
like my grandfather and father before me,
I've been playing with them for years,
spitting them out like sharp-tasting herbs.

I do it because I have no aptitude
for baking cakes or changing timing belts.
I know that I couldn't spend my life
fixing pipes or rearranging gears.

What I do is no better or worse
than what others routinely do
to enable themselves to remain sane,
attentive and relatively alert.

I certainly don't do it to calm my nerves.
My neck and lower back stiffen
and twinge fretfully whenever I
sit down to string together the words.

No, I write because of a peculiar need
to clear the bile that runs deep in me.
Not doing it is not an option here:
it only makes the craving worse.

Spring is around the corner

The snows are going,
the streams are flowing.
Possibilities are everywhere.

Currents multiply and divide,
so under rocks nothing can hide.
Everything races like a hare.

Below the greening hills,
snowdrops and daffodils
outdo the gorse for flare.

The world is shifting fast,
shaking off the icy grasp
of winter's wheelchair.

Spring is around the corner
like little Jack Horner
pulling out a plum or pear.

Young men who are preening
woo women daydreaming.
Love is in the air.

The water that's melting
leaves arable fields swelling.
Opportunities are here and there.

The lively lambing season
says goodbye to wheezing
and cupboards that are bare.

The bees are humming,
woodpeckers are drumming,
heralding in a new era.

An imperfect world

Perfection may be a perfect word.
But it causes a lot of imperfect things:
a perfect storm, a perfect murder
or that hollow feeling when the bell rings.

I quit my own pursuit of perfection
long ago when it nearly cost me my life.
I was so busy trying to be flawless
I almost lost my health, my job and my wife.

My perfect mind was always a tortured one.
So was my perfect body.
Now I strive for 80 per cent of my goals,
and think it a miracle if I can achieve 20.

I never carved a perfect turn
or baked a perfect cake.
And coaches who tell you to give 110 per cent
really need to give their head a shake.

The ancient Greeks' pursuit of perfection
still makes for useful university fodder.
But the Germans' obsession with the perfect race
led millions to the slaughter.

There is no such thing as pure perfection.

All we can do is to try our best

in the best of all possible worlds,

and stop forever beating our chest.

How to ruin a dinner

The other day I dined with an old friend
and everything was going well
until we started to talk about global warming,
then it descended into hell.

It's the same with Britain leaving Europe,
many can't seem to disagree
without attacking each other personally
or launching a yelling spree.

A divergence of political opinion is little more
than a difference in, say, clothes.
It says something about where you're coming from,
but it's a thorn, not the whole rose.

So why do we get so heated about
viewpoints that differ from our own?
And why does it seem to matter so much
that we humans are not all clones?

My mother used to say, when going for dinner,
never discuss sex, religion or politics.
But if you can't talk about what tickles your fancy,
life's a pretty dull bag of tricks.

Besides, in a world where everyone's an expert,
polishing your skills in a debate
should enhance and enliven the conversation,
not pepper it with hate.

The problem is when we're so self-centred
and believe that we're so bright,
we forget there are various sides to every issue
and that no one is always right.

Life is not a numbers game

When people ask my wife and me why we have only one child,
I tell them their interest in our private life has been duly filed.
I remind them having a family isn't a game of deuces wild,
and if one person is special in every way, who needs five?

I also tell them our son, himself the father of two,
doesn't mind being the single standard-bearer for the crew
or having the full parental spotlight trained on his hairdo
without anyone else to substantially filter the view.

He's never complained to us about lacking a sibling,
or feeling desperately that someone is missing,
though the pressure at times must be blistering
to be our sun, our moon... our everything.

Swimming safe in a sea of dysfunction

Let me tell you the story of two brothers,
one a hoarder, the other a neat freak.
One couldn't chuck things out of his house,
the other wouldn't put stuff in.

The two were insufferable together
when they met at their respective homes.
And when they chatted over the phone,
they either had not enough to say... or too much.

So an intervention was sorely needed,
which, for the hoarder, meant a house clean-out
by the same multi-disciplinary team that helped
the neat freak with his sad lack of furnishings.

The mental aspect of the brothers' relationship
was far harder to address in any meaningful way.
The hoarder prided himself on having a clear head;
the neat freak preferred keeping his cluttered.

And when they finally agreed to discuss all this,
they couldn't decide where the tete-a-tete should be.
There was far too little room in one house,
and way too much space in the other.

They eventually opted to meet half-way
in an airy but cosy, downtown café
that was ideally suited to hug the dividing line
between being too wide open and too shut in.

The physical part of the meeting went swimmingly,
even though the brothers didn't shake hands
for fear of spreading contamination.
They kept a safe distance from each other.

It was the mental part that was the problem.
Their words came out either like a dripping tap
or a full-on flood. Bursts of fitful chatter
were followed by awkward bouts of silence.

The moral of this sorry story is that
you're never alone in your dysfunction.
There's always someone as sick as you
or someone who is your polar opposite.

So however you decide to fill your life,
don't carry too much baggage. Or too little.
Then, you won't be burdened with too many
expectations... or paralyzing preconceptions.

And if it is a long-lost friend
you summon up the nerve to meet,
only to find you have little in common,
show some brotherly love. Then move on smartly.

Secret places

Every house, I think, should have a secret room
where adults can hide and little ones play.
It should be shaded from the sun's glare,
but with an airy feel, the opposite of a tomb.

Every house should have a hidden staircase
for dodging hellish barbs and other harsh words.
It should connect via a secret tunnel
to somewhere far beyond the rat race.

Every house should have a secret garden
latched shut behind an ivy-clad wall,
boasting a magical profusion of roses
and rabbits, so it doesn't look too spartan.

Every house has dirty little secrets,
hiding what remains of its shadowy past.
It should have a way of giving them up,
without recriminations or disabling regrets.

Every human needs private places
where no one else is allowed to go...
soothing places that shield them
and help them heal, through God's good graces.

Life's a gamble

You could say I'm a gamblin' man,
I make my money wherever I can.
I like to buy low and sell high,
and intend to do so until I die.

Mr. Market, he's such a hard master,
he gets you to climb aboard, then drives you faster.
He knows where you are vulnerable,
he'll bash you right underneath the table.

You're up one moment, then you're down.
He treats you like a stupid clown.
He's your pimp and you're his whore.
He's always got you wanting more.

Some folks they won't play the game,
they sit tight to avoid the shame.
But you can't win, if you don't take a chance
or appreciate life is one big dance.

Pull the lever, roll the dice.
Shake that pinball, slake that vice.
You won't drink from the lovin' cup
when your bones are broken and your number's up.

Quality

Quality is a hot dog with onions,
grilled just the right way.

Quality is a stroll on the beach
on a sunny day.

Quality is a great haircut
done with no delay.

Quality is a well-stitched wool suit
with almost no play.

Quality is whole-bean coffee
in a no-frills café.

Quality is a chocolate cake
on your best birthday.

Quality is a tender kiss
in a mountain chalet.

Quality is knowing when and how
to make sweet hay.

Quality is the memory you have,
whatever they say.

A modest proposal

Growing up in what's been called genteel poverty,
I dreamed of a mansion with a myriad of gables
overlooking land as far as the eye could see,
with room for a string of horses in the stables.

It was grand enough for an avenue of poplar trees,
a hedge maze to mesmerize visitors from London,
a garden planted with flowers friendly to bees
and a barn where all the cattle could come.

It was a welcoming home where on a busy day
you could watch the sheep being sheared
or host rehearsals for an outdoor play
before taking tea as the evening neared.

It was a place where the vapors of the ages
would mingle with the gales of youth
along a labyrinth of passageways
in a Downtown-Abbey-like drama of gritty truth.

But I found, as I took on an active wife,
that wishful thinking turned into reality.
And a smaller house and leaner life
were far more in line with actuality.

A comfy home with modern plumbing
and well-lit, uncluttered, open-plan rooms
was easier to manage and more becoming
than one with a million silver forks and spoons.

Upsizing began to make no sense,
even when children raised their princely heads.
There was no need to keep up the pretense
that we were a clan of thoroughbreds.

Raising an upright family did not require
us to have the whole village fawning over it.
We didn't need to act like the entitled squire
to convince others we had lives that counted.

We hiked the local hills and dales,
dropped in on hidden fishing holes,
picked tulips, bluebells and daffodils
and petted our share of emboldened foals.

We jumped into various events at the village hall,
baked biscuits and picked flowers for the church,
played cricket on the green and football,
never leaving other people in the lurch.

We left no monument to our passing.
We amassed no troubling mountain of debt.
There was no feeling that we were fasting,
just living the simple life without regret.

Looking back on it now, we laid a strong foundation
for the freedom of which poet Horace spoke.
It was the kind that stems from a life of moderation,
unburdening us from the world's heavy yoke.

Word drama

Words are subversive things,
they act like little bee stings.
They agitate, torment and taunt,
then prick you where you don't want.

That's when they get snooty,
they grow all fresh and fruity.
They don't know when to stop.
Suddenly, they're into hip hop.

They jump around like chickens,
pecking away like the dickens.
They can never just sit still.
It's like they've taken some pill.

Words do get on my nerves,
they're such wily saboteurs.
They needle more and more,
they're troublemakers to the core.

Words are bouncy, jouncy things,
they go up and down like swings.
I wish they'd learn to calm down
or just head on in to town.

I say words have history.
She says they have herstory.
They never ditch their derivations
or their awkward associations.

I'm so tired of their pretension
and nagging condescension.
They should stick to the theatre
where they can mimic Shakespeare.

If I'd my way, there'd be no words,
only the chirping of the birds.
Words bring such bad karma.
I hate their non-stop drama.

A lion's mirage

We're walking by the ocean,
slipping, sliding over the rocks,
aiming for the sunny headland,
avoiding life's hard knocks.

We sight a powerboat surging
over the shimmering waters,
with a lion-like figure emerging
from the captain's quarters.

We stare at the raised stern,
bewitched by its v-shaped wake
as it veers behind the point
without any sign of a brake.

Scrambling over some brambles,
we're hungry to eye the crew,
but the shape-shifting big cat
has vanished from our view.

We look for a hidden berth
where the craft might be tied up.
We see nothing except seagulls
soaring in a shoreline gust.

We realize we've been deceived
by the haze of a classic mirage.
However, we can't help but feel
we've received a clear message.

Don't waste time watching,
gazing at life from afar.
Borrow the heart of a lion
and board a shooting star.

The wise heron

A shaggy Great Blue Heron
materializes out of the ether,
perching on a giant rock
amidst the gravel of the seashore.

Perfectly camouflaged for the grey
panorama of the Vancouver inlet,
the stick-legged, pointy-beaked bird
patiently eyes the Pacific sunset.

Five thousand miles away,
my 99-year-old mother
is perched in a UK nursing home,
waiting for her next supper.

Rail thin, she's always had
boundless energy to burn,
whether hiking in the Dolomites
or tackling some domestic concern.

Family members have flown far away,
but she's still the foundation stone
of their fragile struggle for life...
as the sun sets on her own.

Living large in Legoland

Some say living large is living easy,
spending freely, all they want,
never having to feel squeamish or queasy
about dining out daily at the restaurant.

Others say living large is swinging for the fences,
going for home runs wherever they can,
not engaging in false pretenses
about their next major step or game plan.

Most feel living large is living boldly
playing the Good Samaritan,
helping out the damsel who's lonely,
doing the right thing whenever they can.

Eco-activists see living large as living light,
cutting carbon emissions to save humankind,
basking in the beauty they view as their birthright
and leaving no mess or litter behind.

Rudyard Kipling thinks living large is living decently,
keeping your head while others are losing theirs,
acting moderately and with integrity,
never wavering, never putting on airs.

Living large is not so much what you do
as how you do it... and with what heart.
It's realizing there are things greater than you,
and that love and deep friendship are what last.

Living large is absolutely not taking advantage
of every ruse, racket and loophole you can.
It's the joy you create and the good you manage,
that's what makes you a truly big man.

The aspen grove

If I ever got to rewind my checkered life,
it would be back to when I was 20,
herding horses on the Teton Mountains,
high above the old White Grass Ranch
in Wyoming's jaw-dropping Jackson Hole.

My daily routine as a ranch wrangler
was to roll out of bed in the morning twilight,
grab a waiting pony from the barn corral
and ride out to round up the other ranch horses
overnighting far off in some alpine meadow.

My mount was a slick black steed called Shilling,
and we were soon zigzagging up the sagebrush trails,
our ears pricked for the bells of grazing horses
drinking in their last moments of freedom
before we wrangled them back down home.

The granite peaks soared thousands of feet
without foothills to interrupt the view.
The mist rose from the valley floor where
the Snake River twinkled, the moose wallowed
and the pronghorn antelope still roamed.

It was early fall and the elk were starting to bugle,
the trees were turning from green to gold.
We halted by a grove of aspens, balanced between two worlds:
above, the wild world with sheer crags thrusting skyward,
underneath, the warm one, inviting and mellow.

I was a young man with everything to look forward to --
a university degree, a rosy-looking career
and a young woman who could overlook
my awkward stance and adolescent angst.
She didn't seem to care if I ever hit the mother lode.

But even then I knew I'd never be richer
or sit taller than in that saddle, surveying
the waking earth steaming in the sunlight below.
Nor would I ever feel freer than among those aspens.
I was master of the universe and at peace with the globe.

Horses for courses

Multi-colored Mustangs roaming the American West,
white horses galloping on a Camargue beach,
dark horses prancing in the Namibian desert,
they free me.

Race horses busting out of the gate,
jumping horses flying in the stadium,
hunting horses running with the hounds,
they move me.

Bucking horses in the rodeo,
dressage horses in the arena,
plow horses on the farm,
they drive me.

Horses for courses is what they say.
Horses for hope is what they are.
We read them, they read us.
Their eyes join ours in age-old harmony.

The noble spirit of compromise

Waving signs, stamping feet, screaming and yelling,
insulting your enemy, bashing your friend,
that's what passes for political debate these days.
It's sick, corrosive and it's time for it to end.

Whatever happened to sound judgment and sweet reason?
Whatever was wrong with meeting someone halfway?
Why do we always wind up with ugly extremism?
Since when is badgering and berating others okay?

Why are our politicians so rigidly committed to division
on such major issues as healthcare and immigration?
Why do they apply the tactics of the Spanish Inquisition
to climate "heretics" and others with whom they disagree?

Political theorists have blamed this viciousness
on the never-ending American election cycle.
But I think the pollution is more fundamental,
trickling down like venom from smug, overpaid elites.

Universities have responded by donning ideological blinders,
outlawing critical thinking in favor of everything PC.
In their snowflake world, only one viewpoint's permitted,
the one that sucks up the most taxpayers' money.

Their students have been brainwashed into thinking
that mindless activism and adolescent anger
are how to tackle even petty topics. They loathe
diversity of opinion and the free exchange of ideas.

It's time, though, to stop acting like schoolyard punks
and start engaging in discussion that's civilized.
Saving the planet or draining the swamp will mean squat,
if we don't return to the noble spirit of compromise.

The Montana cabin

Somewhere out there in Montana
is a log cabin circled by wild flowers,
with views of the stately Rockies
that are simply immense.

The cabin has been empty
since the late 1960s,
when it was part of a dude ranch
later swamped by the elements.

As a horseman, I've come to relish
riding by that stubborn shack
and its old pot belly stove
stamping its historical presence.

I've been especially aware of it
since learning a ranch wrangler
once killed a girl he took there.
Their spirits still haunt that residence.

They'd left a ranch party together,
somewhat worse for wear,
to see the pony the cowboy kept
behind the cabin's snake fence.

She came from a rich Philadelphia family,
he from the local Indian reservation.
They were a fetching pair,
their chemistry easy and intense.

She was enjoying summer vacation
after her final year at high school.
He'd ended a tour of duty in Vietnam.
Guiding dudes was how he convalesced.

She'd won every school prize she could,
but saw in him the wild side she missed.
He'd taken the wrong side of the road
and wanted to reverse that trend.

He said he hadn't meant to murder her,
just wanted to constrict her neck
to stop the screams from her Madonna-like face.
At least that was his court evidence.

He'd been a machine gunner in 'Nam,
spending sleepless nights in the jungle
where the heat and smell of death
heightened the suffocating suspense.

He'd witnessed the rape of a village girl
by three GIs -- one of whom raped him.
He'd self-medicated with marijuana
and suffered post-traumatic stress.

The jurors showed no mercy to the marine.
They nailed him for aggravated murder.
Once in the pen, he hanged himself.
He was just 20 when laid to rest.

The mountain ranch never recovered
from the spotlight the tragedy brought.
It was sold to the National Park Service
and lost its warm western essence.

But the cabin still marks the spot
where young lovers traded love and hate.
It reminds passing horsemen that
life never really makes much sense.

Hope stone

Chipping away at the rock,
I carve the jaw, the nose, the eyes,
the arms, the hands, all to size,
aping the rhythm of a clock.

Tick, tock, tick, tock.
I breathe deeply as I struggle
to clear out the rubble
and create human stock.

I envision a lively silhouette,
a soldier presenting arms,
a preacher belting out psalms,
a dancer doing a pirouette.

I yearn for a shape in stone
I can put on a pedestal
and turn into a spectacle
worthy of occupying a throne.

I seek a symbol that is strong,
though it speaks of suffering --
one that looks like a noble lion,
but sounds like a sweet gong.

Paradise

I often wonder what it would be like
to have as much money as I wanted
in my savings account at the local bank.
My only problem would be how to spend it.

Well, naturally, I'd like some kind of house,
but not one so big that I'd be work-bound,
nor one so small that having relatives to stay
would feel like rush hour on the London Underground.

A gorgeous mountain view would be a must.
So would pasture for the horses to frolic,
a cornfield right out of the Field of Dreams
and bird-friendly trails that were gently hypnotic.

I'd have a lawn as smooth as any billiard table
with a Harry Potter treehouse and hedge maze,
plus a gazebo for the occasional tete-a-tete
and Cedars of Lebanon, of course, for shade.

I'd opt for a combined living and dining room
with a cathedral ceiling of high-strength composite.
There'd be antique beds where lovers could rollick
and, for my Italian suits, a huge walk-in closet.

I'd engineer an easy flow from one room to another,
setting it up so robots could do the housecleaning.
I'd ensure the delighted owner didn't have to do
anything too demanding or demeaning.

I'd also create a well-lit study and panic room
where, like persecuted priests of old, I could hide
when unwelcome agents of the state came calling,
or take a secret path to the woodland outside.

Decorating such a hallowed haven should not be an issue;
chic interior designers could do it themselves.
But I'd have the best music, finest paintings
and fanciest books gracing my voluminous shelves.

How would I name this sturdy, stone-built pile
with its cypress avenues, shrubs for butterflies
and all-season flower gardens bursting with color?
I'd call it home. But you could call it paradise.

Rules

Honesty is always the best policy,
except of course when it's simply
an excuse for rudeness and cruelty.

Humor always lightens the mood,
except when it's just a cover
for being offensive and crude.

Dogs are always man's best friend,
unless they bark incessantly
or bite you in your face or back end.

Houses always increase in value,
unless the market in them overheats
and down and down it drags you.

There's always an exception to every rule,
unless that rule has an exception,
then the rule itself becomes the fool.

Everything in life comes with conditions.
We cannot depend on absolutes,
even those rooted in rock-hard traditions.

Our best hope for a light undimmed
is occasionally standing our ground
and sometimes bending with the wind.

Village people

Across the graveyard, the bells jangle
at the west end of St. Peter's Church.
A pack of litter pickers is on patrol,
making short work of any "grot spots"
that fellow volunteers may have missed.

This village isn't as farm-based as it was;
animal smells are no longer in your face.
But the pub's new owners are motivated,
and the heat is on to pretty up the verges
of this pushy Britain-in-Bloom finalist.

Big-city journos and social engineers
continue to predict rural depopulation
will kill off the dove-cooing villages.
Hedgerows and bridle paths, they say,
mean little to the modern urban tribalist.

Their forecasts, though, ignore centuries of evidence
that at heart the British are village people.
They're wired to bolster their beloved hamlets
with a tenacious spirit of togetherness
that in big cities gets crushed by big politics.

Pumpkin-carving parties, bulb-planting sorties
and scarecrow contests aren't everyone's cup of tea.
But villages still give stressed taxpayers a second home
and retired citizens a second shot at life...
with an appeal to the soul that's hard to resist.

Goodbye, dear four-legged friend

My wife and I lost a dear friend the other day.
We still can't believe Kyra has left,
silently, stoically dying at our feet
as a vet squeezed anesthetic into her neck.

A robin called, a crow squawked
and a bald eagle watched over it all,
while the cold, clear light of winter
passed through her undying soul.

Two years after being kicked by another horse,
she was unable to rise in her stall.
Her knees were swollen, her body sore,
her back was literally up against the wall.

Kyra had mixed breeding, with Thoroughbred
and Dutch Warmblood in her veins.
We could see she was something special
even before we took up the reins.

A large chestnut with a kind, liquid eye,
she came to us from an Alberta cattle ranch.
She had a well of inexhaustible energy,
an athlete's body and an over-sized heart.

Like any sentient being, human or horse,
she had her share of faults and quirks.
She could be scarily skittish and fearful,
but was rarely spiteful or malicious.

The most amazing thing about her was
just when you thought you were her judge,
she was judging you on where and how
to give her a pleasurable nudge.

This human-friendly filly soon became
a mare who was a joy to ride or lead --
unless you nodded off into complacency,
then she could make your nose bleed.

Over the years, she developed into a fine
boss mare and all-round character horse
who never lost her fire and passion
for full-throttle gallops and suicide halts.

Some people say horses lack intelligence
because their brains are unnaturally small.
Yet even a foolish human can figure out
they're the size they need to be, and no more.

Humans travel now in cars, planes and trains.
Their bond with horses, though, remains as before.
Fewer people may ride, but those who do
have equine partners they adore.

If there is a horse heaven, Kyra is there
where the sight of her flowing hair
and the sound of her flying hooves
are like thunder and lightning in the air.

Minding my time

I said to my wife the other night
I'm in the homestretch of my climb,
I really have to do something with my life,
because I'm running rapidly out of time.

She said stop being such a crybaby,
you can still flip a nickel and stop on a dime.
In fact, you can do anything you want,
you just have to show some spine.

I reminded her of a couple of dead newsmen
who were work colleagues of mine.
I bet they didn't know their days were numbered
before they met their final deadline.

My son called the other day from Montreal.
He's a young father in his prime,
but he said he was feeling stuck in his career
and feared bells were starting to chime.

I said I thought that way when I was his age,
and still think so from time to time.
The fact is, whether you're eight or eighty-eight,
you're always one misstep away from dying.

My amazing mom turns 100 next year,
if the stars and her health align.
She still dreams of the great family get-together,
and has done so since the dawn of time.

The other day, I bought a new wrist watch.
It has four dials that tell the time.
I try to make sure they all keep ticking.
Any pause could be a warning sign.

Life is a dangerous, one-way journey.
To survive it you need some discipline.
But you don't need to live every moment
as if perched precariously over a land mine.

The smartest way to hedge your bets
against the cruel ravages of time
is to be a good person whenever you can.
That way things tend to work out fine.

Skating on a sea of superficiality

Don't judge a book by its cover is what we're always told.
Yet that's what we always wind up doing, blowing hot or cold.
Whether candidates seeking office or movie stars chasing glory,
we always assume the best or worst of them, not their true story.

We look at their hair, assess their jawline and nose.
We size up their accent and eye the brand of their clothes.
Then, confusing their outer with their inner being,
we pigeonhole them based on the skin tone we're seeing.

We're drawn to movie puppets squeezed into tailored suits
or image-addicted dictators mouthing platitudes.
We crave the packaged look and the political poppycock.
Plain speaking is as popular as a skunk or smelly octopus.

Honesty, modesty and rationality are all fine qualities.
But they're foreign to those who convince us their policies
will lead to the land of milk, honey and TV reality.
We, meanwhile, continue to skate on a sea of superficiality.

Mr. Go-Get-'Em

The man who talked on TV too much
really didn't have too much to say.
Instead of provoking intelligent discussion,
he'd just grab the nearest cliché.

You couldn't call him a pukeworthy presenter.
Yet he rarely thought things through,
using his trombone voice to get out of trouble
when his fulminations proved too good to be true.

His hair, teeth and posture were above average.
But his trademark was his rah-rah expression
of the need for viewers to pursue their dreams:
"Go get 'em, gals and boys, don't forget 'em."

Around the TV station, he kept his upbeat manner,
though he had few supportive work friends.
His colleagues tended to tune out his blather,
infinitely preferring MSNBC's or CNN's.

Not that they held his verbal diarrhea against him.
They knew he was a chip off the old block,
that his father was a talkaholic shopkeeper
whose sales pitch would never stop.

However, everybody did pause to wonder
why his ratings had reached new heights
right before his vocal cords ruptured
in an explosion of fractured sound bites.

The station now has a charming new presenter,
economic with words, quiet as a church mouse.
There are many viewers, though, who still miss
Mr. Go-Get-'Em, the ultimate blabbermouth.

They may have resented how he courted the camera
and bombarded them with his gobbledygook.
But they felt at heart he was one of them.
He didn't simply play it by the book.

Hometown tourist

So often when I try to drive downtown,
the tangled traffic is a total downer.
I get flustered, then frustrated
by how easily I manage to flounder.

Motorists with a trigger middle finger,
cyclists who refuse to move over
either cause me to be mildly bipolar
or turn me into a full-on monster.

But crossing the bridge the other day
to Vancouver's mountain-ringed harbor,
I decided to adopt a chill new attitude
by striving to be a bit of a charmer.

Pretending we were on summer vacation,
my wife and I joined out-of-town visitors
soaking up the sunny Pacific panorama
and anything else that riveted us.

We drank a cup of joe on a viewing bench,
watching buzzing float planes take off in style,
while busy tugboats and tankers chugged along
against the backdrop of a glowing sulfur pile.

Moored at the port's cruise-ship terminal
was an ocean liner called The World.
It sported a dozen decks of luxury to keep
owners of its 165 "residences" unperturbed.

People are able to stay aboard The World
for as long and far as they wish to sail.
It has a tennis court and all the trimmings
for a hedonistic life on a grand scale.

But you don't have to roam the world's oceans
to shoot the breeze... or sniff it like a celebrity.
Try instead being a modest hometown tourist,
you might be amazed at how much you see.

Sweet cider

I've always been rather greedy for life.
But as I get older, I get greedier.
I want to snatch all that comes my way,
even if it makes me that much needier.

I never thought I liked politics.
But now I spend hours devouring it.
I follow every little twist and turn
as if it's a fly and I'm swatting it.

I used to have no time for houses,
figuring a tent and backpack was all I needed.
But now I'm a slave to TV shows about
kitchens being rebuilt and lawns reseeded.

I once had little enthusiasm for sleep,
viewing it as so many wasted hours.
But now I long for a firm mattress
as I would a bed of fragrant flowers.

I used to have no feeling for birds,
at least those of the feathered kind.
But now I reach for my binoculars
whenever they're wheeling in the wind.

I once had little taste for meals,
save those with baked beans and soggy chips.
But now I'm pickier about my food
than any piker playing pick-up sticks.

I used to think of love as something
you did in the seat of a pickup truck.
But now I've learned that, if you listen
to your heart, you will be moonstruck.

I once had little interest in death...
less, in fact, than in aging rust.
But now I know that we all must,
as chimney-sweepers, come to dust.

I've always been rather greedy for life.
And as I get older, I get greedier.
I want to snatch all that comes my way,
making sweet cider out of lemonade.

Let the good shine through

We're all built a little one-sided,
we all lean to the right or left.
We all lack a degree of balance
or have faculties that are otherwise bereft.

So stop being so blue.
Be kind to yourself and true.
Always give others their due.
Let your good side shine through.

We all have our Achilles heel,
we all have a tragic flaw.
We all have spots we must cover
or disorders that are appallingly raw.

So stop being so blue.
Be kind to yourself and true.
Always give others their due.
Let your good side shine through.

We all have unwieldy bodies,
we're all too short, fat or thin.
We all could use photo-shopping
or straighter posture and a firmer chin.

So stop being so blue.

Be kind to yourself and true.

Always give others their due.

Let your good side shine through.

We all suffer setbacks

or bouts of frustration.

But that shouldn't end in scowling

or wallowing in terminal stagnation.

So stop being so blue.

Be kind to yourself and true.

Always give others their due.

Let your good side shine through.

Laying the table

If you build it, he will come.
But what if it gets built, and he doesn't?
What if he has better things to do
than hang around an Iowa cornfield?

We witnessed that the other day
at our local conservation area,
where every effort's been expended
to create a Field of Dreams... for birds.

We trudged around the muggy mudflats,
past several strategic viewing points.
Yet we saw no birds or ducks at all,
not a cawing crow or a squawking gull.

They say you can lead a horse to water,
but you can't make him or her drink.
You can't force God's creatures to be your buddy;
they don't come with a magnetic strip.

Birds come and go where they need
to feed, socialize and preen their feathers.
They appear uninterested in the
laser-like attention of human suitors.

It's the same with humans who yearn for love.
The worst thing they can do is turn
themselves inside out by being too needy,
too available or too deferential.

Instead, they should gently lay the table
and draw folks deftly to the feast.
Looking desperately for love is for losers;
it's best to let it slowly spread its wings.

Self-righteousness

We live in a knee-jerk world.
We go left, right, right, left.
Like the fascists and communists of old,
the more we hate each other,
the more like Bobbsey twins we become.

We live on a tribal planet.
We go right, left, left, right.
How rational and decent we are
rates far less on the virtue scale
than the race or gender we belong to.

We live in an Internet era.
We go left, right, right, left,
where the medium's the message
and the content doesn't matter.
It's just a stream of fake-news chatter.

We live on a planet of fear.
We go right, left, left, right.
We're paralyzed by the Eco-Apocalypse,
terrified the world will end
because we didn't pay off the climate gods.

We live in a self-righteous world.
We go left, right, right, left.
We smash blindly into each other
to prove that we were right,
even though we're destroying ourselves.

True North

In the North, everything is bigger.
Bears, black flies and beer bellies
are so big they make everywhere else
seem positively Lilliputian.

Canada's three northern territories alone
make up four million square kilometers.
If you add the 1.7 million over which Alaska sprawls,
Texas doesn't seem so crazy big at all.

Big-city planners say shoe-box apartments
are needed to house Earth's dense population.
But the only true density in the North
resides between pin-headed politicians' ears.

I once spent Christmas in a tent in the North,
lulled to sleep by a Robert Service poem
about the northern lights and the rush for gold
on the haunting "roof-pole" of the world.

I live in a one-bedroom apartment now,
parking my econobox in a numbered bay.
They clean the windows, cut the grass,
check the alarms and haul the trash away.

But to this day, I never venture into the snow
without recalling the vast northern wilderness —
and the yearning for space that still drives
diehard risk-takers to live the big life there.

Unison

The universe is expanding exponentially
or multiplying, dividing and contracting.
We're only a moment in time away
from the Big Crunch, Big Rip or Big Freeze.

Alternatively, the astral anatomy
may mushroom out forever
into the void, as experts suggest,
with baffling synchronicity.

The cosmos, I think, mirrors humanity,
and will end with a big bang
or puncture at some juncture.
I'm already sensing how it will be.

My own life started as an anomaly,
a misshaped preemie with matted hair,
reliant on a hospital incubator,
fighting, screaming like a banshee.

Expansion possibilities grew royally,
though they were never limitless.
I had good and bad schools, so-so jobs
and an unerring instinct for disharmony.

I married and had a healthy baby
who became everything I was not,
an engineer with unbounded dreams
and a passion for astronomy.

I passed the career torch to him recently,
retiring because of chronic debility.
And as my stress level changed,
so did my personal philosophy.

I came to appreciate more fully
that life will end when it wants,
that the way to skirt senility's fog
is to embrace the miracle of geography.

Every morning the sun rises in intensity,
every evening it sets peacefully,
laying out an elaborate feast
with riotous disdain for symmetry.

Full-time workers mightn't agree,
because their struggle for survival
depends on having tunnel vision
and being a bit of a busy bee.

But when aging commits its grand larceny,
the colors fade, lines blur, words wobble.
Present moments merge with the past
like starving pirates in a stormy sea.

Retired folks realize that relatively shortly
after they begin to sleep the Big Sleep,
it'll be the universe's turn to reach the limit
of its own desperate dissonancy.

They learn everything there was and will be
will eventually contract, as experts predict.
Matter and space-time will collapse
into dimension-less singularity.

Mind, body and spirituality
will reduce themselves to a lone point.
The three will become two and the two one.
We will all become one... eternally.

God's country

Horse and rider move as one
as they traverse a Teton mountain meadow.
You can track them with binoculars
as far as the lodgepoles will allow.

The sorrel horse is young and willing.
The cowboy, sitting tall and straight,
eases his mount along the trail
with a rhythmic diagonal gait.

I lose them as they inch up Death Canyon
past the pretty Phelps Lake Overlook.
I'm sure they'll overnight at the cabin
near the grove of Engelmann spruce.

Ringed by a palette of wildflowers,
marmots straddle rocks dating back eons.
Beside the creek, moose feed on willows,
ever leery of bears and mountain lions.

The canyon, it's said, is named after a
surveyor who hiked in and disappeared.
And venturing into dizzying country like this,
it pays to be ready for the worst.

Rider and horse know they're out on a limb,
but dodging demons to them is second nature.
They also know they're that much closer
to the finest work of the Creator.

Lost freedom

I never learned much at university;
there was too much else going on.
But what I did vaguely grasp was that
it was okay to have a contrary opinion.

Now, universities strive for the great group-think.
They want everyone to talk and write the same.
Challenging uniformity is never permitted,
if it hurts someone's feelings or causes shame.

Universities profess to love diversity of race and gender.
Yet they seem to detest differences of view,
especially about climate change or reverse discrimination.
Anything politically-incorrect is taboo.

Logician Bertrand Russell said men fear thought
as they fear nothing else on earth.
Albert Einstein said blind belief in authority
is the greatest enemy of the truth.

Essayist Anais Nin said when we blindly adopt a religion
or political system we become automatons.
So why are universities so intent on turning
energizing journeys into mindless marathons?

Liberty-loving John Stuart Mill said silencing
of free expression is especially evil.
Yet, sadly, to our higher-purpose institutions
he's just another dead white male.

I never did learn much at university.
But I came to appreciate higher education
is not what it indoctrinates you with.
It's what you did during your summer vacation.

Sadness

Sadness is straddling an endless buck fence
on a lonely stretch of sagebrush in the Rockies.
To one side, hazy rivers meander
forlornly through the valleys of lost time.
To the other, mountains are still left to climb.

Sadness is rubbing your face in the mirror
and waking up to the spiteful presence
of the lines, scars and greasy creases
that deliver the expression you deserve
when kneaded together or otherwise combined.

Sadness is a lament for paradise, lost
through a series of physical and spiritual
deformities and debilitating deficiencies.
It never quite went the way you expected it to,
you never quite rose out of the slime.

Sadness is owning up to your current condition,
while lauding the luck that landed in your lap,
along with the loose network of loved ones
that on occasion still rises to the occasion.
Ignoring them would be a serious crime.

Sadness is realizing where and who you are
and who and where you will be until eternity
are the inevitable outcome of your own humanity.
There is no point in blaming yourself for the fact
that the sun will set and the bells start to chime.

Perfect beach

Sipping a Mai Tai on a tropical beach
is for many the height of satisfaction.
But I think it's at least as appealing
to hug the shore in a less obvious location.

I love to go where the cobbles are so rough
that only those with hard-soled shoes
and a passion for the unknown will go
in search of seclusion and wild, open views.

Give me a beach where the ocean wind
whips the waves onto the log-strewn shore,
discouraging party crashers and other
upstarts from slipping through the door.

Give me a spot where the smell of the sea
runs into little or no competition,
with nothing else to excite the nostrils,
certainly not coconut-scented suntan lotion.

Let the only strident noise be that
of a raucous crow, Great Blue Heron
or seagull swooping to snatch a shellfish
it then drops on the rocks to crack it open.

Let the faraway view be that of a freighter
barely moving on the hazy horizon,
carrying its cargo to remote lands
under the gaze of a mirage-like mountain.

For many, the perfect beach is a lazy stretch
of soft white sand kissed by turquoise waters.
I prefer one that may be hard to reach,
but tickles the heart of tenacious travelers.

You'll always be part of me

I first saw you 60 years ago
when you were a little girl
and I was a little boy
acting in the school Mikado.

You liked playing hide-and-seek;
I much preferred Conkers.
But whenever your head poked out,
I gave it a knowing peek.

During our awkward teenage years,
you were a wary, watchful girl
who worked harder to fit in
than to elicit laughter or tears.

But your eyes lit up at the hunt ball,
sharing snapshots of you and your pony,
a strikingly handsome combination
feted and envied by one and all.

We went to separate universities.
Yet, I clearly recall you visiting mine
when its gardens were a riot of color
and we swapped sun-kissed memories.

You landed a job in the City
as a high-flying financial analyst.
I flew to North America to find myself,
thinking you were sitting pretty.

You got married in the fall
and I didn't bother to reply
to your wedding invitation.
I didn't want to address it at all.

I mined the land of milk and honey.
You raised two lovely children
in a trendy London row house
and a cottage in the country.

Only when your divorce was final
did you come to my Canadian cabin.
We walked past golden aspens
when you said you felt suicidal.

We next met at a friend's apartment.
My grey hair matched your pallor.
We laughed, though, when we recalled
dancing the Dashing White Sergeant.

Later, you languished in a hospital ward
where I clung stiffly to your hand.
Your brave, wide smile, though,
struck just the right chord.

You were always my guiding light,
my main point of reference.
So why then is life so cruel
to those who do it right?

Yours is the love that set me free.
Yours is the life I might have led.
All those years we were out of step,
but you'll always be part of me.

The brightest month

Wisteria climbs the farmhouse walls;
glowing buttercups line the trail.
Frank the organic farmer is planting his tomatoes;
Doug, opposite, is reaping his first cut of hay.

Cyclists are gearing up for the Tour de France,
or whatever torture midsummer brings,
and there's still a ton of snow on Mt. Baker
in spite of all the climate hysteria.

But the light shines brilliantly in May,
striving to drive the relics of winter away,
reassuring dough-faced doubters
summer is just around the corner.

Or maybe it's trying to convince worrywarts
the world won't end any time soon,
as they might believe on hearing the latest
salvo from Trump or Kim Jong-un.

Nothing is more certain in this world
than death and taxes, so they say,
or more hazy, foggy and uncertain
than long-range weather forecasting.

But in a contest between our planet's rhythm
and the spin cycle of the political swamp,
I'd pick May's darling buds and nature's seasons
every bird-chirping, sun-drenched day.

My corner-store friend

We knew each other when
our lives were still half-empty.
We were high-energy soccer parents
whose sons played on the same team.

We liked to argue over everything
from human-caused global warming,
which I didn't go along with,
to smoking, which he still believed in.

We used to run into each other
at the local grocery store,
which smelled musty, but had parking
that was easy for maneuvering.

Once while we were gabbing there,
we agreed it'd take at least 25 years
to learn what truly was worse,
climate change or cigarette inhaling.

The years passed like second-hand smoke,
but finally I returned to the store,
only to find it boarded up and ringed by
burst bags and other signs of littering.

I paused for a minute in its parking lot
to reflect on the half-century
since my proud soccer-parent days,
and wondered how it had been for him.

A little later, I ran into a mutual friend
who divulged it hadn't turned out well:
My old pal was hiking with his son
when a boulder crushed both of them.

It was a brutal reminder that time
changes all, including the corner store.
But human life still is as fickle
and cruel as it's always been.

February is the cruelest month

Brazen earthworms surfacing
on a rain-soaked pavement.
My wife cradles them one by one,
before plopping them onto the grass.

She cares about worms, snakes
and other slithery creatures.
I much prefer to keep them
at a respectful distance.

One person's Good Samaritan
is another's busybody
whose ruthless meddling makes
matters worse for everybody.

Chairman Mao and Joseph Stalin
claimed to care about the people,
but killed millions more of them
than rulers who didn't give a fig.

T.S. Eliot prays God teach us
both to care and not to care.
And I agree there's much to be said
for learning simply to sit still.

So often humans use caring to
wriggle out of doubtful behavior.
I just wish those wet worms
could tell us what they think.

Solo in the snow

Everything is near,
crisp and clear.
The snow is here.

The dogs are playing,
horses are neighing,
the snow is weighing.

I sight a mourning dove
on the phone wire above.
The snow is my love.

I gasp in pursuit
as I pick my route.
The snow is mute.

The footing is heavy
in the copse already.
The snow is confetti.

A lonely gnome,
I push on home.
The snow is foam.

I attempt to sleep,

but can only weep.

The snow is deep. The snow is deep.

Twitterverse

A haiku

Hold tight, brave poets,
Donald Trump's tweetstorm mimics
crows in attack mode.

Rhythm

The setting sun lights the peaks,
glowing dramatically.

The wind bends the Douglas fir,
blowing relentlessly.

The Canada geese swan by,
honking insistently.

The boots crunch the sand,
tromping decisively.

The tide moves out,
ebbing inexorably.

Nature rules the planet,
rhythmically, ruthlessly.

Sucker for eco-variety

I live an environmental activist's nightmare
right across the water from an oil refinery.
Yet I wouldn't change my home location
for all the coal in India and China.

I love the way the 50,000-barrel-a-day facility
puffs clouds of water vapor during the day
and lights up dramatically at night
like an intricately laced Christmas tree.

But then I like a mix of nature and nurture,
not just endless greenery, however climate-friendly.
I've never been one for vast tracts of forest
or vast tracts of anything, however virtuous.

What time after time works for me
is a tangy blend of the wild and the domestic,
of urban, suburban and rural scenery.
I'm an absolute sucker for variety.

If people say brick, I say stone.
If they say mountain, I say valley.
If they pick a fir, I choose a maple
or a grand cathedral over a pristine canyon.

You could call me an unrepentant contrarian,
or at least someone who's easily bored.
What I do know is I hate the sameness of things,
especially if they look drab and barbarian.

Let's just say, when it comes to the environment,
contrast is for lions and consensus for lemmings.
Humans may have a primeval urge to think alike,
but modern minds shouldn't take early retirement.

Under your nose

We went for a hike today
amidst a snowy mist.
My wife of 41 years and I
rock-crawled and reminisced.

Sailboats bobbled in the water,
mountains winked and watched.
Along the familiar trail,
we all played our hopscotch.

A robin grabbed its worm;
we nibbled at a bag of chips.
There was nothing unusual
about our respective scripts.

Make it new, the pundit says,
try what no one knows.
The best bet, though, is often
right under your own nose.

Down the trail, my wife and I
did something we couldn't resist.
Leaning on a big old fir,
we hugged ... and we kissed.

Recipe for damnation

We live in an era of change;
we're from a generation of rage.
What kind of stubborn mange
has driven us to this stage?

Muslim radicals want to blow us to hell,
governments to tax the air we breathe.
Our choice is to be hurled down a well
or have a cleaver cut us off at the knees.

So, we've handed over the reins of power
to a bully-boy, reality TV star.
Sweet reason has flown out the door.
Madness reigns like a wrecking bar.

We live in an age of self-expression,
from a generation that strikes a pose.
The fact is the lingering recession
still shows the emperor has no clothes.

So-called holy and political wars
have mauled the world for thousands of years.
It's time we took a different course
or at least started to change gears.

Old people can't pay their heating bills;
young people are starved of decent shelter.
Yet weasel politicians boast of their skills
in stopping us from becoming warmer.

The eight richest men in the world
are as wealthy as half its population.
How can we say this is well-deserved
and not a recipe for damnation?

Wooden wisdom

I went to the local park the other day
to see the birds and dogs at play.
A memorial bench faced the wind-kissed sea,
with a plaque saying: "Skip, jump, laugh, pray."

Other benches from other family members
praised those who'd completed their life's duty
before shuffling off this mortal coil,
radiating peace, joy, love, beauty.

They were loving husbands, caring sons,
tireless moms and doting daughters
who, when they weren't rocking the cradle,
were paddling bravely through troubled waters.

One striking message lauded a lively logger
who, moments after being heard telling
park visitors he had the world's safest job,
was crushed by an old cedar he was felling.

"In loving memory of Chip 'Chopper' Lawton.
Tragically taken from us, aged 23.
Fallen too early, but never forgotten.
Rest in peace on this seat beside the sea."

Laugh, pray, skip, jump.

A wooden bench honors a cocky young buck

cut down in his prime doing what he loved.

Pity, though, he couldn't have kept his mouth shut.

The false god of guilt

Whatever he does, wherever he goes,
the white man's guilt has become his burden.
He likes to think of himself as especially enlightened,
but all he's created is a bitterly divided world.

Working stiffs try to do their best for their families,
while having to pay off rapacious governments.
So why should they feel bad about refusing money
to Middle East warlords bent on maiming each other?

What is there for these workers to feel so guilty about?
Did they create the rivers of blood that flow in desert lands?
Did they bring the dust storms and plagues of locusts?
Hell no, despite what professional revisionists say.

You might have thought the 9/11 World Trade Center bombings
would have drawn people together in collective self-affirmation.
Instead, the so-called developed world's twin obsessions
consist of breast-beating and other self-flagellation.

Wallowing in the plight of peoples in far-flung places
may satisfy the desire of luvvies for self-dramatization.
But it diminishes the centuries-old struggle for freedom,
for which our guilt-free forefathers so selflessly fought.

A big old tree with shallow roots

Husband, father, brother, son.
Wrangler, trucker, hired media gun.
In an otherwise unremarkable career,
I've played many roles, downed much good cheer.

The Yukon, Alaska and big-sky Montana,
Ireland, Scotland and beautiful British Columbia
are where I've climbed mountains, forded streams,
scouring the landscape in pursuit of my dreams.

But despite marathon days and sleep-short nights,
I've never hit the jackpot or corralled the northern lights
or developed those grand, life-long passions
that fill the cravings restlessness fashions.

Colleague, crony, partner, lover.
Joker, dodger, talker, drummer.
I've always tried my darndest to do my best,
but too often have wound up hunched and depressed.

I'm like the big old fir tree with the shallow base
that the wind blew down recently near our place.
Gnarled, bug-ridden, with needles of faded green,
it forced hikers to turn back from the forest stream.

The question now is not where I'll spend the next morn,
but whether I too will be beaten back by the storm,
or still have the guts to take one more test...
and the will to dig down deep before I rest.

Visit to Cates Park in North Vancouver

I walk on the grassy bank overlooking the shell-filled beach
and view the gulls and crows wheeling in the fall wind,
fearlessly going wherever it takes them,
and I ask where has all our courage gone?

I take in the giant, white-painted anchor
commemorating where, in 1792, British and Spanish explorers
first arrived in these mountain-ringed waters,
just down from what later became a lumber mill.

I examine the plaque marking the squatter's shack
where Under the Volcano author Malcolm Lowry
used to ply his tortured trade.
What drove him? Fear of failure 5,000 miles from home.

I view the smoothly-carved five-tonne hunk of jade
that serves as a strangely fitting memorial to those
who fought in the war to end all wars
for the freedoms we enjoy, even here so far away.

It's a sharp reminder of how timid we've become
and how far more fearful we are of giving offense,
especially to those who too easily take it,
than in taking a stand... come hell or high water.

Elusive love

A sonnet

We like to think we can fix up our friends
with a girl or boy who excites their deepest desires.
But all too often we lack the skill or sense
to help them find the passion that never tires.
University professors don't offer such courses;
they leave us to muddle through the best we can.
Parents are worse at picking the right sources;
mutual delight is not part of their plan.
TV matchmaking shows are guilty pleasures,
with brassy bachelors and bachelorettes
scrapping like hyenas over blood-soaked treasures.
In real life, it's tougher to earn those epaulets.
Most of us lack the fidelity of a turtle dove.
And nothing is more elusive than true love.

Drinking the climate Kool-Aid

The more enlightened we think we are,
the more extreme we become.
From Islamist thugs to Greenpeace punks,
angry zealots struggle to replace democracy
with something far more loathsome and odious.

Some embrace death like a desert blanket.
Others hug spotted owls and polar bears
and wolves and whales and garden snails.
None seem to give a hoot about humanity.
They just want to enforce their beloved "consensus".

The earth's been around for billions of years.
Its climate has always been changing.
So do these eco-cultists really believe our
governments can, with a flick of the switch,
turn down its temperature a couple of degrees Celsius?

Carbon dioxide may help warm the world,
but it's far from the demon it's deemed to be.
It gives our planet life, feeds the plants and trees
and is a powerful weapon against poverty.
It doesn't taste, smell... or make us nauseous.

If pollution is bad, make the polluters pay
directly for the harm they inflict
on mountains, fields and streams.
Don't pardon them with medieval carbon-offset schemes
that appeal only to the greedy or gormless.

Feverish climate researchers have drunk the Kool-Aid
when it comes to agonizing over the apocalypse.
They've massaged stats, manufactured hockey sticks
in their pursuit of grants and glory.
They're invariably petty, peevish and pretentious.

The best scientists keep an open mind.
They don't label doubters "deniers".
They're also not so vain as to think they've
uncovered the universe's darkest secrets.
They're much more cautious and conscientious.

Comedian George Carlin wasn't joking when he said
it's absurd to talk about saving the planet
when we don't know how to care for ourselves.
Yes, human lemmings are what worry me,
especially when they're sure they've all the answers.

A happy ending

We're on a path to destruction,
we came from a passage of pain.
It's silly to expect life to be plain sailing.
All we can do is our best to stay sane.

So don't obsess on one aspect of your being,
your looks, health or fame,
or you might miss out on peace and freedom.
And that would be a great shame.

Pushing ourselves in pursuit of excellence
can be rewarding and bring great acclaim.
But perfectionism is invariably destructive.
It often brings little but self-blame.

Even struggling to unlock the secret to
happiness is bound to bring great strain.
So aim to live a tranquil life like Epicurus
and strive for something more tame.

Leave a light footprint on life,
and cheerfully, gracefully play the game.
Excessive self-love and self-loathing
are like hypochondria; they're heavy and lame.

From a happy hour to a happy ending,

the definition of happiness has always changed.

Aristotle called it the highest good, to which all our actions aim.

Thomas Jefferson thought it a right, like a property claim.

But a recent study of UK women found happiness

isn't as powerful as some people proclaim.

It doesn't make us healthier or live longer.

Happy or unhappy, we meet our maker just the same.

Convoy of change

Change arrives like a freight train
with a full load of coal.
My heart is pounding.
So is my shriveled soul.

From where I'm standing
on the platform's edge,
I feel the ground grumble
like Satan's over-loaded sledge.

I'm wheezing desperately
as the asthma takes hold,
squeezing my spirit,
forcing my lungs to fold.

I hear the train whistle
clear, insistent as a bell.
It's coming directly
to take me straight to hell.

The train runs right over me.
I don't have time for fright.
A giant gas lamp explodes,
flooding the world with light.

The smoke fades into thin air.
The train leaves the station.
I'm breathing more freely now,
ripe for transformation.

But all I see are false prophets
calling me to arms,
pitching a mirage of truth
in a desert devoid of charms.

Politicians dangle shiny baubles
to sucker passengers in.
Yet their platform is bombast,
their dogma a mortal sin.

Priests proffer a heady cocktail
of ritual and sacrifice.
Their message is sadly dated.
So is their unctuous advice.

Eco-shamen exhort us
to hug rolling rivers and trees.
Their creed, though, is anti-human.
Their hypocrisy reeks of sleaze.

The real convoy of change is
driven by forces beyond their hide.
Restless travelers should go with it...
and buckle up for the ride.

The Consensus Kid and Kim Jong-un

I'm the Consensus Kid.
I follow the crowd wherever I'm bid.
If they say "jump," I say "how high?"
If they say "no," hell I won't go.

I know better than to buck the trend.
I try to find a group in which to blend.
Parroting what teacher said
is how I've always got ahead.

I'm the Consensus Kid.
I follow the crowd wherever I'm bid.
If they say "jump," I say "how high?"
If they say "no," hell I don't go.

When it comes to politics, I have opinions,
but I prefer those that belong to millions.
I have no sympathy for the minority
who fail to genuflect to authority.

I'm the Consensus Kid.
I follow the crowd wherever I'm bid.
If they say "jump," I say "how high?"
If they say "no," hell I won't go.

Big Brother is always watching you,
so why bother having a different view?
I mean, when all is said and done,
Kim Jong-un is number one.

I'm the Consensus Kid,
I follow the crowd wherever I'm bid.
If they say "jump," I say "how high?"
If they say "no," hell I won't go.

As for climate change, there's no debate,
unless you yearn to make Al Gore irate.
But if you seek a juicy grant,
upsetting the apple cart sure ain't smart.

I'm the Consensus Kid,
I follow the crowd wherever I'm bid.
If they say "jump," I say "how high?"
If they say "no," hell I won't go.

You may think we consensus kids
are conformist little PC prigs.
That's cos we hate to cause a fuss.
We'd much rather climb aboard the bus.

I'm the Consensus Kid,
I follow the crowd wherever I'm bid.
If they say "jump," I say "how high?"
If they say "no," hell I won't go.

You say lone wolf, I say sheep.
You say leopard, I say Little Bo Peep.
There's no reason to go against the grain.
All you get is a world of pain.

Breakdown

Life just wears you out.
Believe me, you'll know it.

All that you've been and done
goes straight down the toilet.

You wake up one morning
with nothing to show for it.

Your body breaks down,
you can't postpone it.

The shell you see in the mirror,
you won't dare expose it.

You forget what you had
before time stole it.

Your memory's wiped clean,
don't try to decode it.

Tapping on your computer
won't make you a poet.

Life grinds you down,
you can't control it.

All you can do is gently
download it. No shit.

Aging cool

Every plant has its season,
every dog has its day.
But why do we reject reason
in our painful attempts
to keep old age at bay?

Humans are pushy creatures,
fearful of others getting ahead.
But why fixate on fashion features
we fancy will convince others
we're a budding thoroughbred?

Humans are beasts in love.
We pine for that divine person
who'll woo us like a little dove.
But must we babble like a baby
in desperate need of diversion?

Humans are higher-purpose people
hard-wired to embrace a church
or other structure with a steeple.
We're hooked on seeming virtuous
and hate to be left in the lurch.

Humans are huge second-guessers,
who always crave another shot.
But life's all about current pressures,
so live it coolly with composure...
and leave it while you're still hot.

Focus

At a certain stage in life,
memories flutter away
in a flurry of forgetfulness.

Relentless time distorts
and discards them, as rust
devours our mental processes.

We either mark their passage
by letting them slip into the void
or bless them with our focus.

We concentrate those recollections,
flawed as they may be,
into one moment at one location.

We choose, say, a mountain place
where the wind is gentle
and the ravens are calling.

We pick a spot where we can see
other peaks, with valleys,
bridges and roads in between.

Then, with one panoramic sweep,
we bring together all we've done
and all we've dreamed of doing.

We sort out the highs and lows,
and the dicey parts in between,
without guilt or gloating.

We don't gloss over what went on,
but we don't detail it so much
that it reads like a master ledger.

We celebrate and seal it with
the clarity that surrounds high places
where destiny meets destination.

Then, we distill all that was
and all the joy and pain it brought
into one fine, light libation.

We drink it slowly down into
our creaking waste system.
We breathe... and breathe again.

About the Author

Cambridge-educated Jon Ferry has worked as a correspondent for Reuters international news agency, a columnist for the Vancouver Province newspaper and a reporter for the Toronto Globe and Mail, the Edmonton Journal and the Victoria Daily Colonist (now Times Colonist).

He's covered every kind of story from the Olson murders in British Columbia to the Mackenzie Valley Pipeline Inquiry in the Northwest Territories, the Exxon Valdez oil spill in Alaska and the drug war in Colombia.

Arguably, though, the happiest times of his life have been spent with horses and horse-loving people in Wyoming, Montana and British Columbia.

Made in the USA
Lexington, KY
22 December 2017